Coping Using My Silly Imagination

A child's point of view.

Gotham Books

30 N Gould St.
Ste. 20820, Sheridan, WY 82801
https://gothambooksinc.com/

Phone: 1 (307) 464-7800

© 2024 *Sylvia Yvette Del Angel*. All rights reserved.

No part of this book may be reproduced, stored in a retrieval system, or transmitted by any means without the written permission of the author.

Published by Gotham Books (August 28, 2024)

ISBN: 979-8-88775-839-8 (P)
ISBN: 979-8-88775-840-4 (E)

Because of the dynamic nature of the Internet, any web addresses or links contained in this book may have changed since publication and may no longer be valid.

The views expressed in this work are solely those of the author and do not necessarily reflect the views of the publisher, and the publisher hereby disclaims any responsibility for them.

Coping Using My Silly Imagination

A child's point of view.

by

Sylvia Yvette Del Angel

Hello, my name is Leilani Olivia and I am four years old.
I want to share some of my thoughts and silly adventures with you.
Let me show you.

I live with only my mommy now, who do you live with?

I used to live with both mommy and daddy but we moved away and now live in an apartment. We were living with mommy's cousin but all the big kids would always close their doors in my face when I tried to follow them to play. That made me really sad. All I wanted was to be part of their group. We did not stay long there. My mommy was able to get a job to get us our own special place to live.

Now it's just us girls. I love our spacious new place. I can run and not have to worry about bumping into furniture at all. My mommy and I even sleep in our sleeping bags on the floor and it feels so fun. We even watch tv together in my little DVD player. I do miss my daddy though. My daddy is a Marine and he is not around much. He is always busy traveling and working. I miss him so much and I think my mom misses him too. Do you ever miss anyone?

At times, when I am not busy, my feelings confuse me. I can be mad, sad, and happy all at the same time. Sometimes I get so mad and I make a big mess. My mom gets mad at me but she tries her best because she was in the military too. I think they are trained to notice little things.

How do you clean up your messes? I try to hide it under my bed, but my mom always finds it when she is looking for my shoes.

I get so cranky and I don't know why. Do you ever feel that way? Crazy feelings really upset me and I pout and cry. I do not realize sometimes I just need a hug or for my mommy to hold my hand. I get tired of crying and some days instead of crying, I find a way to feel better. Anything helps, even playing with simple things like sticks and crayons. I sometimes just hug my mom or tell her I need love. It always makes her smile and my heart feels good when I see that.

During my games at home, my mommy does not understand why I spread my toys around to have fun. I sometimes also spread lipstick all around my face because it feels good. I feel that I need makeup to look beautiful for my friends and I can't help it that I ruin her lipsticks.

My friends like to move around a lot and it is not my fault that accidents happen. I told my toy turtle to sit down and not to get in the sink as I washed my hands, but he insisted on jumping in. Why do I have to get in trouble for splashing the mirror and leaving water everywhere? Do you ever get in trouble?

How can I talk to my mommy when at times she is sad, mad, and happy? I am not sure which mood she will be in when I tell her my friend spilled the milk all over her library book. I think I will hide away so she will not find me. I am so sad. I need to figure out what to do to help me feel better. What do you do?

I guess I better go color and not say anything just yet.

Coloring is another one of my favorite activities that gets me super excited! I color things my imagination helps me see. My drawings take me to worlds that have many trees and colors. I call my favorite places colored forests.

In these forests, I sometimes see witches, trolls, and monsters.

Sometimes the things I see are mean and sometimes they are funny.

Even though the things I see are scary looking, I am not scared. Some monsters make me laugh and tell me funny jokes. I laugh really loudly and talk to them silently. My mom chuckles because she knows I am using my imagination.

Once I get tired of playing, I quickly run to my mommy so I can cuddle with her. Cuddling is my favorite and I feel good hugging and kissing my mommy. It makes me happy when my mom pays full attention to me. It makes me feel really special.

Sometimes during our special moments, I tell my mommy I miss daddy. I'm comfortable telling mommy about how I feel. Mommy understands me and hugs me tighter. Hugs from her help me calm down and work out my confusing feelings. Have you ever told your mommy or daddy or loved one that you just need a hug or some attention? It helps me, I hope it can help you. My mom told me she cannot read my mind. I just laughed but I know it is true so I try my best to tell her about how I feel.

When I am sad, my mommy notices and pays attention to my feelings. I like to draw for her and show her my friends. I like being noticed and I like feeling loved. My favorite time is when my mommy talks to me and spends time with me. Happy feelings make me feel like a baby kitten. It is important for me to know that I am loved constantly. I also tell my mommy I love her every time I feel loved. It makes her smile and that makes me happy. Have you told anyone that you love them? I also tell my mommy when I do not want a hug. My mom respects me and asks for my permission when she wants a hug.

My mommy is always there for me, I know it because she shows me by not lying and always being there for me when I need her. I also see it when she tells me something and actually does it for me. I know I am safe with her, emotionally and physically. My mommy loves me.

I remember when I was a baby in diapers. My mommy would drop me at pre-school and I would cry. I would cry because I thought I would never see her again. She would always tell me she would be back for me, but it was hard for me to understand. At the end of each day, she would always do what she said. Her actions taught me to believe her and develop trust. I love how my mommy continues to come pick me up from school every day. I love you mommy.

I am still little now but I know I am growing. I am able to do more things all by myself without help sometimes. I do like being able to ask for help when I need it without getting in trouble. I sometimes do have to breathe in or count to five in my head if I get inpatient or angry. It's hard to grow up sometimes. I guess I can use my imagination again while I wait to get help. Help meeeeeee mommy!

I know my mommy and daddy still do there best even though they are not together. I do not understand that part yet, so for now I'll just paint and tell my mommy when I need more love. Why do all these feelings have to be so confusing? Please help me understand it mommy! I try my bestest, just don't give up on me mommy. I love you always mommy. Please be patient and hug me, mommy. Look mommy, look at my beautiful life I drew for you.

PART II
6 Years Later With New Sister

Hi! My name is Norah. I'm 9'years old. I live with mommy some days and with daddy on other days.

That's my kitty, Mustard. He does what I do when I am frustrated. Changes were not easy for me, and I would cry and hide in any corner. Sometimes I would kick and scream. I am still learning to be ok with changes since I now have two homes. In my new home I would create hiding places with blankets, boxes, or a little tent. My mom would let me keep my spots in the living room because she noticed it helped me. I loved to hide my favorite miniature toys and anything special to me in my very own space. Why can't I just have one home like before? I do not like changing so much. That makes me feel frustrated! Let me tell you about my story.

I used to cry a lot because my mom moved out of the house where she lived with me and my dad. Her apartment was really loud outside, and I could hear it inside. The apartments were close to the street, and you could hear ambulances, fire trucks, police, or people driving really fast. My other house was not loud like that. All that noise scared me, and I did not like it. My mom would help by playing music and dancing or by playing funny cartoons that made me laugh.

I would have a hard time knowing how to think right or ask for what I needed. I really could not breathe right, and I would cry really loud and throw myself on the floor while I kicked. I really did not like to feel that way and my mom helped me by learning about crystals and different shapes of rocks. I would get a crystal and feel it to see how I liked it. I liked how cold it would feel and how pretty it was.

Sometimes I would take my mom's make up cases and put them inside. I liked the way they looked in their tiny homes. When my mom would find out she would get upset and start yelling my name but then I would also notice her breathing deeply and would sternly tell me to ask next time I wanted something of hers. Taking from my mom wasn't always a good idea so I then started to take things from my older sister. She would also get mad and yell at me so then I would just hide and stay in my tent.

My mom would notice that I wasn't really coming out of my tent so much so she started to show me other things that I could do. She brought me this little bowl and showed me how to make sounds using a wooden Stick. She told me she used it to help her breathe and relax after working all day. I liked making noise and helping her relax by making soothing sounds from the sound bowl. I also tried to put away the bowl, but my mom asked me to leave it somewhere where we can all use it. I agreed and that made me feel ok.

I did not always feel ok. Some days my mom would clean my corner and I would get mad because she moved my things. I really would get so mad that I would just jump up and down and scream. My mom would remind me that it's ok to be mad but to make sure I breathe and use my crystals to help me feel better. She always said, "Did you look at your crystals, did you feel the smoothness or rocky surfaces? She also said, "Did you hear the sound from the sound bowl? She would then ask me; did you eat your snack and drink your water? "If you are hungry or tired you won't be able to make yourself feel better." I would then laugh and say, "that's true." I sometimes just wanted to hide in my little corner with my toys. I needed to feel safe knowing some things won't change after I put them there. My mom would also ask me if I needed a hug. I would say no a lot so she would just say ok and leave. Sometimes I would change my mind and I would run to her, and she would squeeze me and tell me she loved me. I would then ask her why she left my other house.

My mom would tell me she left my things in my other house where my dad lived so that I would feel safe. She bought me other things at her home for me to use. I did like the comfort of knowing I had my things just like when she was living there. I always wanted my mommy, but she would tell me I needed my daddy time too. I could not understand. She would tell me to breathe and pray when I feel sad. She would remind me to use my words and say no when I needed to. She would make me feel safe and would hold me when I would say yes to a hug. She would also respect me when I wanted to be in my little tent. I liked having my little area that no one would bother me in.

Now I feel more comfortable with having to stay with my mom sometimes and then my dad, but I still need my own space and privacy to feel safe.